The Erotic Sculpture of India

Text and Photographs by
MAX-POL FOUCHET

Translated by Brian Rhys

The Erotic Sculpture of India

CRITERION BOOKS NEW YORK

PUBLISHER'S NOTE

The dates of Indian history lend themselves to some controversy. In this English language edition we have naturally decided in favour of the chronology generally accepted in England. Therefore this version shows several differences from the chronology usual in other countries.

© 1957 La Guilde du Livre et les Editions Clairefontaine, Lausanne
English Translation © George Allen & Unwin, Ltd, 1959
Library of Congress Catalog Card Number 59-6127

Printed in Switzerland by Héliographia S. A., Lausanne

Introduction

When Indra, King of the Gods, had destroyed the Titan who held the waters of the earth captive in his entrails, he returned to the heights of the Central Mountain with the song of the rains and running waters in his ears. But where his dwelling once stood, he saw only ruins and ashes. So he summoned Visvakarman, god of works and arts, and asked him to build another palace to match his powers. The architect set to work; soon towers, buildings and gardens rose among lakes and woods. Indra urged him forward impatiently. Each day he called for some fresh marvel, new delight for the eyes, walls more imperial, pavilions more richly adorned, statues greater in number and cunning. A fever seemed to burn in him. And Visvakarman, exhausted by his labours, decided to lay a complaint before the Creator of the world. Brahma received him, gave ear, approved, and went to plead his cause before Vishnu, the supreme Being. Help was promised.

Soon a young Brahman appeared at the King's palace and demanded audience. Charmed by the light of his eyes, Indra granted his request. "Oh King," said the messenger, "thy palace shall be the noblest of all." These words were sweet to Indra's ears, and he rejoiced. Vishnu's messenger continued: "It shall be the noblest of the palaces which the Indras before thyself sought to build." The King became uneasy. "Dost thou say that there were other Indras, other Visvakarmans before ourselves, other palaces before mine?" "Indeed yes," the youth answered. "I have seen them. Moreover I have seen the world arise and vanish, arise and vanish again, like a tortoise's shell coming out of Infinite ocean and sinking back. I was present at the dawn and the twilight of the Cycles, past counting in their numbers, nor could I count all the Indras and Visvakarmans, even the Vishnus and Brahmas, following one another without end."

Perhaps there was a shadow of doubt in Indra's astonishment. The messenger simply pointed to the ground of the audience chamber: long dark lines of ants were moving across the floor. "Behold these ants. Some of these for their piety deserved to become kings one day like Indra, to command the gods even, and conquer dragons. Yet these kings were found wanting and were borne away in the ebb and flow of lives; once more they became ants. Oh Indra, how many Indras are there among them, builders also of palaces!"

Thereupon the King repented, recognising that Beauty exists only in deeds. He asked Visvakarman to forget the error of his ways and cease the useless work upon his palaces. He bade farewell to his wife, handed the royal powers to his son, and went into solitude, to transform his vain desires into the single desire for Redemption.

This story of Indra's fault, told at great length in the *Brahmavaivarta Purana* and the *Krishnajanma Khanda,* may serve indirectly as an introduction to the study of Hindu art, and help the reader to approach an order of thought that might seem strange on first encounter.

For it is the pleasure and pride that we should call aesthetic which the King entirely renounces, because the messenger has reminded him of the great verities. These are the transmigration of souls, and the endless succession of lives, in the course of which our deeds never fail to find us out and decide what our future lives shall be. And to *karma* and *samsara*—our deeds and reincarnations—there is also added *moksha,* the need for Release by union with the Divine.

Such then was Indra's fault: an ardent longing for decorated palaces, which showed that he was under the spell of images and charms, of the manifold appearances of Illusion (*maya*). Renouncing illusion, Indra passed into the desert to purify himself and seek the one and only Being.

But there was another fault. Indra's proud monuments should have been dedicated to Release. The king had failed to see them as props and supports for meditation, helping beholders to become one with the Absolute. Mere aesthetic enjoyment (which is our enjoyment since Western art so strikingly lost its earlier religious significance) was in Indra's case not only foolish but alarming in prospect. His diversion from the true path was fraught with dangers. In his eagerness for loftier walls and chiselled stone, he showed what perils lie in wait for those who become slaves to *maya* in all its vigour and profusion, and do not master it.

While we should only see an architect intent on beauty, the Brahman becomes uneasy in his mind, fearing that art may lose its true significance. For art belongs in a twofold sense to *maya*. First by the nature of its works; they are only cunning and magic, illusory like everything which is not the One. And further, creative art images and reflects the energy of *maya*. Illusion is equivalent to a dynamic transformation of the primal substance. It makes the undivided manifest by dividing it. *Maya* not only causes the One to become manifold, but is itself manifold by its very nature. And as our minds cannot dwell on the diversity of things without becoming forgetful of the first principle, so every work of art, belonging as it does to the world of manifestation, must resolve itself into a truth of such light that its own forms shall be consumed. For no work of art, however perfect, is an end in itself; it is only a means—means to release.

Illusion must cast out illusion.

All this does not prevent the work of art (as the rites of caressing will show) from being the house of the god and a concrete aspect (*murti*) of the god shaped as idol. Form is indeed a manifestation of the formless. And this only seems a paradox, for the formless is the source whence all forms flow. The temple, having its source in the undivided, can be absorbed into it again when the faithful use it to free themselves from illusion. For then it serves as *yantra,* an active means for meditation, offering at the same time an image conveying the relationship between the worshipper and the godhead, between this world and the celestial.

Art was invented so that Truth might be clothed in form for those who cannot see it in naked essence. So art is the servant of truth and even points to truth and, in so doing, betrays its own nature.

Art, in other words, is never *separate.*

As its purpose is to direct the soul, Hindu art must reject the freedom which we have allowed to artists as of right since the close of the middle ages. The artist is more an interpreter than a creator. If he followed his own imagination in devising shapes and forms he would be committing the sin which has disturbed certain divines of the West, a sacrilege in fact which was condemned by St. Thomas Aquinas in these words: *Si quis appeteret creare caelum et terram, quod est proprium Dei, quod in appetitu esset peccatum* . . . So the artist is an image-maker, and his art a craft. It was not in the East but in the West that men found themselves faced by a contradiction between Church dogma and the beauty of many works, and formed the notion of art. And it has often been pointed out that there is no equivalent for our word *beautiful* in India's vocabulary.

The rules by which the artist worked gave him no freedom except in the more mundane treatment of erotic themes, as we shall see. And these rules apply not only to divine beings and events; there are even laws *(sastras)* which formulate the aesthetic. Beauty is achieved by accepting certain specified limitations *(pramanas).* The work of the artist obeys principles and norms that guide the architect's T-square and the sculptor's chisel, respects that talent for codifying and classifying which is characteristic of India. And the

artist instinctively responds. In his work breathes a loving acceptance of faith *(bhakti),* also shown in the prayers and acts of self-purification that he makes (or used to make) before his hand reaches for the tools.

The Hindu artist mirrors Truth. His mind's eye sees first, before he looks upon this world; his vision directs and confines our gaze. Not that he rejects illusion's shapes and forms, for these he must use to please, invite the gaze, bend it towards the truth. For Indian art is not abstract. It can powerfully express the formless in shape and line, since its models, the gods themselves, are only passing manifestations of the One. And so it is that the symbolic form of the temple consumes its own symbols. Surcharged with statuary below, gradually the building strips itself of adornment in its upward climb until it culminates in the sparest of finials, itself an emblem of that pristine drop, the first germ, source of the whole Universe.

A ritual art of this kind has its dangers. There is the risk that it may become too repetitive and lapse even in its classical age into excess or dead formalism. The mind's eye eventually becomes blind to living visual forms.

But it would be a mistake to underestimate the role which Hindu art assigns to feeling *(bhava).* Works of art must be moving, must be infused with the dynamic of transfiguration. It may be helpful here to compare the language of form with the Indian idea of poetic language. Each word in a poem has three meanings— literal, figurative and suggestive, these last two being quite distinct. In the same way a piece of sculpture might be said to have its literal and figurative meanings, proceeding from rules and guiding principles. But it also suggests another indefinable quality. This indefinable something we can call the flavour *(rasa)* which is just as essential as mere obedience to rules. And without this flavour perhaps Hindu art, for all its formal riches, might seem too severely ritual, too far removed from our own aesthetic notions. Fortunately for us, however, the smile that radiates from the stone of Rheims cathedral finds an answering smile on the face of the *apsaras*.

The common touch mingling with the divine—a characteristic of Indian life—can also give their art a naive simplicity on which canons and codes might frown.

This common touch may well come as a surprise to Westerners who have forgotten what carousals sometimes occurred in Gothic cathedrals. Nor is it out of place in a religion whose gods, manifestations as they are of the supreme essence, none the less belong to *maya,* like the world over which they reign. There are certain illustrations in this book showing scenes of divine love-making and human ardours side by side. Art here draws no line between the sacred and the profane. And before passing judgement on many pages, it will be well to remember that the gods also are only disguises of the primordial *Spirit*.

And the behaviour of these gods! Quite often far from transcendental! What with their battling and knavery, their quarrels about precedence and property, there is much that they could teach the gods of Greek mythology. Siva, for instance, cuts off one of Brahma's four heads with his sword and throws it into the Ganges. And the goddess Parvati deceives Siva, her husband, with Agni, god of fire, whom she then hides in her body, just as if it was a wardrobe in vaudeville. Krishna, one of the incarnations of Vishnu, whisks the veils off some cowgirls when they are bathing, gazes upon their nakedness, and bewitches them with his flute-playing. And the Aryan gods might even be charged with racial prejudice, for they refuse to invite the Dravidian Siva to their festivities, yet bow before him in a somewhat cowardly manner when he threatens to wipe out the universe. They fly into a rage, create monsters and set them loose, then wonder how to deal with them when their anger subsides. So they have to join their breaths together and create a goddess to protect them from the buffalo demon.

As for their minds ... Ganesa, the elephant-headed one, is a god much revered, yet his odd appearance is explained by legends that seem peculiarly irreverent. Parvati is said to have created him out of her bodily secretions to put a stop to Siva's vile habit of coming to catch her in her bath. So Siva, in a fury, chops off the guardian's head, and is then so flustered by Parvati's shrill cries, that he claps a new head on his victim, the first that comes to hand, which happens to be an elephant's. But here is another, simpler version: While walking in the woods, Siva and Parvati chance upon an elephant in busy dalliance with his mate. Much intrigued by the posture which nature demands of the female elephant, they decide to change themselves into the same shape. And soon Parvati gives birth to a hybrid son, half man and half elephant.

These tales will help to illustrate the "common touch" and show that there is no division between gods and men, particularly as regards physical love. The amorous prowess of certain gods is sung and vaunted. And the symbol used for such a theme is sufficiently ambivalent to deserve mention here, however much Indologists may frown.

After the universe had been destroyed but was not yet reborn, in that interval between destruction and creation when there was nothing but darkness and water, Vishnu-Sesha was resting in his own substance, shining with latent energy among the germs of the lives to come.

Suddenly at his side a form appeared, of the same vast dimensions and equally bright. "Whence comest thou? What is thy name?" the figure asked. "I am Brahma the Creator." Vishnu denies this: "Thou sayest thou art the Creator. But I am He. And the Destroyer too.

I make the worlds and unmake them." Brahma protests. Vishnu is angry. They argue concerning their powers.

Then a third form appears, of such majesty that they are amazed and fall silent. Soon they see that it is a *lingam* (phallus), the base of which is plunged in the uttermost depths of the ocean of ages, while the top is lost in the clouds. "Let us try and discover whence this *lingam* arises, and where it ends," says Vishnu. Brahma replies: "Dive then, thou, into the deep, and I will reach the summit." Vishnu changes himself into a boar, and Brahma into a gander. One plunges into the depths, the other is quickly lost in the heights. But they are baffled and return. Neither has found an end, for all his powers. Then like a pomegranate steeped in sunshine, the phallus is rent and splits open. Siva appears in the heart of his emblem. "I am your master," he says. "I am the Creator, Preserver and Destroyer." The two other gods can only acknowledge his power. They bow down and worship.

According to the *Markandeya Purana* and the *Kurma Purana,* the *lingam* is of "a fixed and fundamental form," and by comparison all other forms are only passing illusions. It symbolises the creative energy of the male. The emblem has the shape of a short cylindrical stone topped with a rounded cap. As a ritual object it is widely venerated and is to be seen not only in temples dedicated to Siva, but also in the streets of towns, by the wayside in country places, and in private dwellings. The faithful have small models just as the devout Catholic has his crucifix; many wear it as a charm. A pebble smoothed by the sea into adequate form can serve instead of the carved pattern. There are Indians who even refrain from eating eggs on account of their shape. Rites for the *lingam* are simple: it is decked with flowers, washed, anointed with buttermilk, or with sweet-smelling oils.

The *lingam* stands upright on a flat base, the *yoni,* which by its shape—round, oval, polygonal or square—represents the female sex, the matrix. The two are often carved with a realism that cannot be denied, especially the phallus; none the less the *lingam-yoni* has a twofold symbolic meaning. The union of the two gives a direct representation of the creation of the world. Uncompromising in their grandeur, they symbolise Genesis itself.

But this twofold emblem would not take us to the very core of Indian thought if it did not also and above all express the resolving of the many into one. By joining itself to the *yoni,* the *lingam,* the primordial axis, shows that the Absolute is deployed in multiple forms but is again resolved into oneness. Taken as one, the *lingam-yoni* expresses the antagonism of the male and female principles, and then in the triumph of singleness destroys that antagonism. The words "two-in-one" seem quite inadequate to describe this: the fusion is too profound. The world is created in and through diversity, and is dissolved when reabsorbed into the primal germ, just as male-and-female are created different but find their true existence in the very abolition of their difference.

As for the act of love *(mithuna),* it can be represented by copulation without loss of its esoteric meaning. To some copulation signifies the union of substance *(prakriti)* and essence *(purusa);* for others it represents more directly the moment when the self *(atman)* becomes merged through Release with the supreme impersonal Spirit. In a word, copulation figures Bliss.

The *lingam,* or in any case some phallic sign, was an object of worship before the Aryan invasions. Evidence of the cult is traced in many remains dating from the Indus Valley civilization (3000-2000 B.C.). The effigy of a god, perhaps Siva, with the sex in erection has been found in Sind, at Mohenjo-Daro, and we may speculate a little upon this discovery. May it not well be that the emblems of early local fertility cults were given a higher symbolic meaning by the spiritually-minded Brahmans? As it proved impossible to abolish these cults which had flourished since neolithic times, perhaps an attempt was made to incorporate them in a higher metaphysic? Did they gradually undergo change and survive in the Vedic religion? The contempt and even hostility of the Aryan gods for the Dravidian Siva would then be easier to understand. And Siva's rise to ultimate predominance would encourage the revival of the primitive fertility symbols common to most early peoples. There is a significant legend worth recalling, which tells how Siva roused the fervour of his followers at Benares by walking about naked with his sex in erection.

However all this may be, Hindu art was certainly enriched with a wealth of erotic themes beyond comparison. On our Gothic cathedrals such subjects are rare and scattered, well tucked away from the unobservant eye, but on certain Hindu temples erotic themes actually equal images of the gods in numbers. The Westerner who has never been to India and only knows her art through academic works can scarcely conceive how insistent, how abundant they are. To gain some idea of the space sometimes allotted to them, let him imagine one-third at least of the Sainte-Chapelle in Paris covered with such figures.

Official authorities are modest when they describe this art as "sensual." For the truth is, "sensuality" is linked with such obvious representation of the sexual act that the word seems lame and often ill-placed. The bas-reliefs at Khajuraho and Konarak, despite the feverish fantasy of certain postures, are too realistic to be dismissed. The British were well aware of this and often tried to turn tourists away from these places. In 1837, James Fergusson, one of the best English archaeologists, praised the architecture at Konarak but condemned the "obscenity" of the statuary. Mutilations have been inflicted on these reliefs, not always due to the action of time, the onslaughts of storm and the raging floods of the monsoon. The British in their prudishness were at least respectful; the same cannot be said for the fanatic destroying hand of the Muslims, whose seven centuries of occupation went before.

Should we always pass over the realism of these bas-reliefs and consider their symbolic meaning only? Are they in fact always symbols of spiritual union and divine creation? Many would have it so, but it seems to us preferable to make a distinction between those reliefs where charm of form suggests the idea of Release, and others where it would be difficult, if not impossible, to see more than a representation of the most earthly pleasures.

Consider Vishnu's exquisite wooing of Lakshmi at Khajuraho (p. 67). The delicate restraint of the divine palm and fingers, scarcely supporting the breast of the goddess; the pliant response of the incurved bodies, the tenderness of the faces and their serene meditation. Nothing here but speaks of supreme harmony. Here is the veritable *mithuna*: sensual union imaging mystic union.

Then turn to the frieze decorating the base of the temple of Lakshmana (pp. 86, 87). What trace does one find of the harmony, the serene detachment, the grace even of the other work? Here, from right to left, eroticism is crudely paraded in a succession of scenes. Copulation, sodomy, fellatio, fondling and titillation are elaborated in a frieze of carnal pleasure, a gallery of postures, a triumphant orgy.

As one might expect, the sculptor's interpretation of *mithuna* varies according as the subject is god or man. The goddess Lakshmi is not, properly speaking, the bride of Vishnu, nor Parvati of Siva. They are their feminine emanations, and represent the gods' energy

10

(*sakti*) in female form. So there is no dual principle in divine couples, only an expression of essential oneness. The all-pervading monism of Hindu thought is once again affirmed. Siva, indeed, can be represented in a shape that we should call androgynous. In the bas-relief at Elephanta (p. 33), his twofold nature is indicated by the single female breast, and the mirror held in one of his left hands. *Mithuna* on the divine plane is an expression of ineffable joy. This cannot be so with human beings, who are dual in their lives, and couple as the carvings on the Lakshmana temple remind us.

Even as we pass from gods to beings half divine or supposedly so, sensuality becomes increasingly apparent. What, for instance, are we to think of the *apsarases*, those female figures endlessly recurring in the sculptures of India (pp. 16, 34, 42, 43, 44, 49, etc.)? If we accept the authority of Heinrich Zimmer, they represent the seraglio of Indra's paradise. These celestial creatures, singers and dancers blessed with eternal youth and imperishable beauty, dispense the joys that reward the virtues of the faithful. They symbolize the innocence of nature, delight unmixed with tears, carnal consummation free of all remorse and questionings. They are priestesses of sexual initiation, dedicated to the celebration of this mystery and, like the *houris* of Islam, sacred courtesans, promised mistresses of the blest.

Yet if they incarnate sensual love in the other world, the *apsarases* possess all the eloquence of earthly charms. These are unsparingly displayed and exaggerated by posing and bending and twisting, in attitudes which we Westerners normally expect to find in cine magazines. Indeed these suggestive, smirking creatures are the "pin-ups" of spiritual emancipation. Their beauty may promise ineffable joy, but they scarcely smooth the path of approach for the faithful by reminding them of this world's delights. They are ambivalent to the eye, and there precisely lies their role and function.

Ranging down from gods and demi-gods to human kind, the portrayal of love undergoes a change to marked realism. There is no hesitation in depicting physical love in its crudest aspects, though with the addition of various ingenious refinements which in themselves constitute quite an art of the flesh (pp. 56, 60). Postures occasionally involve acrobatics (p. 69, central relief; p. 60*c*); the protagonists even require the help and support of acolytes to maintain their balance. Scenes are unhesitatingly shown in which several people interlace, twine and cooperate. Two women quite often titillate or satisfy the desires of one male (p. 52*b*; p. 57, upper groups). Frequently a third person attends upon a couple's dalliance (pp. 59, 60*d*). There are, of course, many chaster scenes, some of quite touching delicacy (pp. 26, 29, 48, 58, etc.) but in the rest such ardour prevails that these seem to be a mere prelude. Taken in all, they afford an erotic spectacle so varied and definite and compelling as to be beyond any comparison.

During our stay at Khajuraho, a holy man dressed in the yellow robe, with a pilgrim's water-pot in his hand, was eager to show us certain reliefs and details which might have escaped our notice. (As it happened, they had already been pointed out to us on arrival by the village children!) These sculptures, he urged, should arouse disgust; their purpose was to show the evil, the forbidden thing. Popular tradition in Orissa makes another such attempt to justify the existence of erotic friezes on the temple of Konarak. They are said to protect the building from storms and scare lightning away. Far from attracting, they repel.

A very simple and pious explanation! But it entirely ignores the look of contentment on the faces of the "sinners." We must face the fact that the attitude of the artist in these representations of eternal bliss is *indulgent*. At the same time it will be well to bear in mind the views of certain students. M. Alain Daniélou, for instance, suggests that the twenty-four postures of *yoga,* which help to change the subtle centres of the body and so attain harmony, find their equivalent here on the erotic plane. And we can well agree with M. Georges Guette that one would have to become a yogi before attempting to copy some of the contortions figured in stone ! "The *Chhandogya Upanishad,*" he writes, "shows erotic pictures as symbolic equivalents of the mystic syllable *Om.* When the two sexes conjoin, one satisfies the desire of the other; in the same way the syllable *Om,* in the conjunction of its parts, satisfies all desire." In other words, the physical act can be transmuted into a spiritual one. It is performed to effect transubstantiation. Like the syllable *Om,* it becomes equivalent to a Yes or Amen uttered by the lover.

So a work of art depicting the act would thus give a twofold significance to love—on the profane level, but proportionate to the sacred.

There are also reasons for thinking that the character and prevalence of erotic art may vary from region to region owing to local influences. It would be tempting to look for some connection with Tantric rites, but the carnal consummation so often apparent in the bas-reliefs can scarcely be reconciled with a rule of self-control, whereby the orgasm was interrupted to divert its energy and tension towards spiritual ends. So perhaps we should look for influences of a simpler kind.

At Konarak, for example, the friezes may represent a call for renewed fertility in a region where population had wilted after centuries of Buddhist chastity, though, as others claim, the explanation might be found in the mere caprice of a prince. Moreover in the Hindu religion there is, besides paradise, a hell where the soul sojourns awhile after being judged by Yama, god of death. And in the popular mind paradise vaguely blends with the idea of a place of sensual delights and carnal enjoyment. This the sculptors of India would depict for them, just as our western artists portrayed the chaster pastimes of the elect.

For it is our prudery which lends these bas-reliefs an aura of scandal. There is no such feeling in India. We should remember that four motives are recognised in the moral teaching of the Brahmans for human conduct: *artha,* which concerns material goods and wealth; *kama* —desire, passion and love; *dharma*—the intellectual and moral duties; and *moksha*—corresponding to release. Erotic art depicts the second. Also, Kama, god of love, is recognised as a powerful animator of the universe.

These are various explanations, but all show that the iconography of love cannot be divorced from the spiritual and everyday life of Hindus. To veil it would be false.

The Hindu artist, as we have seen, was bound by strict rules and codes when interpreting the higher orders of being, but clearly regains his freedom when he describes —or invents—mankind's sensual delights. We drop then from the loftier regions of symbolism; the realism of everyday life emerges, zest is shown, and sometimes there are touches of fun. When gods are left behind and mortals reappear, art becomes simpler, freer, gains in spontaneity what it loses in hieratic calm. Life swarms. We are down to the level of the teeming market places of India.

If the body is clothed in formal perfection in Hindu art, this does not deny its spirituality. For it is within this frame, this housing, that Release must be sought. This is the place where the manifold merges with the One, where the seen is absorbed in the unseen, where the separate self unites with the essential self. The fleshly body proclaims the beauty of the mystic essential body. It is the ultimate flowering of the primal germ.

The artist expresses this praise by deformation. Women's legs are elongated, hips and buttocks enlarged to emphasize the slenderness of the waist. The breasts have no droop, scorning gravity's law. They are spheres, self-enclosed worlds, attached directly sometimes to the torso underneath, as if they were not carried by the torso, but sprang straight from it, or rather as if the fruits of some orchard never spoiled by the hand of time were grafted onto the flesh to assuage man's hunger and thirst and renew them endlessly. Of Parvati it is said: "She bent under the weight of these twin globes, like a fruit-tree heavily laden."

Grace and passion; a present promise. Cruel, tender *apsarases*. Visions breathed by the divine.

For us who are strangers to the religion of India, these figures may only speak nature's sensual language. Do not let us blush to think of them as manifestations of profane love. For in this world of ours, where the transcendental is degenerating into mere formalism, where higher thought makes base concessions to policy or dubiously compromises, perhaps this love is the last sign of the sacred. Let us not fear to see in these creatures a mirror of our desire. Undoubtedly the erotic in our nature, followed through the ways of art, is a quest of the Absolute.

March 1957   MAX-POL FOUCHET

13

14

Sanchi

(IIIrd century B.C. to XIIth century A.D.)

Acropolis is not a word to be over-used, but it does come to mind when you are at Sanchi and have spent long hours under the harsh sun and the rains, ascending the steep paved walk that climbs from a poor village to the place of Poverty.

A bend in the road, a pond, and the shrilling of children's voices among the women drawing water; then— silence, and the climb up the straight path to the top. There are no propylaea, but you pass through an invisible door, the path becomes gentler, and the body feels as the soul would feel, if it was worthy of Him who offers to ease all burdens.

On the skyline appears a stone circle, and out of this, umbelliferous in space, rises the triple umbrella of the Sage. The hill is in labour; with each step forward the dome protrudes further, the egg of the *Great Stupa* gradually emerges. Then at last the full hemisphere, encircled with tall stone slabs. And here are the tumuli (known

the world over, from mounds in America to Etruscan tombs)—for such are the *Great Stupa* (p. 15) and the lesser ones about it. But these were not only funerary. From the time of Asoka's reign they contained relics of interest. In the modest *stupa* to the north-west (p. 17) lay those of Sariputta and Mahamogallana, two disciples enlightened by the Master. They were taken away to England, and returned to Sanchi in 1952, to be housed in a new and depressingly ugly little building.

Asoka, the "monk-king," a devoted adherent to Buddhism, built the first shell of the *Great Stupa* in the third century B.C., and it was enlarged by the faithful in the century that followed. The cupola is of brick, covered with a sandstone layer, and rests on a terrace that rings it with an ambulatory where processions walked in times past. Today, pilgrims come from China, Burma, Ceylon, Tibet, and chant their hymns and burn their amber sticks.

The *Great Stupa* is still girdled at ground level with fencing in stone, and in this enclosing wall, some ten feet high, four breaches open at the four cardinal points. Before these stand four gateways—the *toranas*. On their pillars and architraves are recorded in admirable carvings the legend and life of the Buddha, his adoration, his lotuses and the Wheel of his Law—symbols guarded by paunchy genii, elephants, and peacocks, symbolic of Asoka.

On this hill, round the first *stupas* and monasteries, others were built over a period of a thousand years. Across the plains overlooked by this citadel passed conquerors—Huns and Muslims. But by the thirteenth century A.D. the acropolis began to lose its followers and was swallowed up in jungle. It re-emerged in 1838 after six centuries of neglect, to mark the sky's approaches with its buoys. From the eastern gateway, under a tree like a triumphal arch, a *yakshi* looks across the years to the *apsarases* of Brahmanic India (p. 14). The fruits above her—and on her—grow at every dawn.

Mamallapuram

(VIIth and VIIIth centuries A.D.)

From the foregoing page to this, from the *yakshi* of Sanchi to this *naga* and his *nagini* at Mamallapuram: six centuries, and India to cross from north-west to south-east, from the Deccan to the Carnatic.

But here there is no slope to climb to a bare hill top, no carved gateways to pass, to step onto the ambulatory designed for meditation. The sea's flat floor lies before us, and the waves come plodding in like pilgrims towards the gods figured in stone.

The sea is at hand; its sand is underfoot; its salt browns and burns the bas-reliefs. From the branching cocoanut trees the children come down, bringing milky water in the nuts. Ships used to anchor here in the past alongside the dealers in elephants and gems. Ptolemy the Greek mentions Mamallapuram in the second century A.D. among renowned ports, and Hiuen Tsang of China did the same in the seventh. Roman coins sometimes crop up on the deserted shores.

From the fourth to ninth centuries the Pallavas, kings and masters of the South, developed sea power, and their fleets carried the truth of Vishnu and Siva to the isles of the Indian archipelago. One of the great Pallavas, Mahendra I (VIIth century A.D.) was according to tradition a playwright, musician and poet. Did the Word give him a love of the imperishable? He would have no building done in wood, bricks and mortar. In the sands of his kingdom great granite blocks lay scattered. Shapes of things to come. They were hollowed and fashioned into temples. Images of gods were carved out of them, and divine events lived in the rock. He began the work. His son Narasimha I continued and completed it. From his reign (c. 642-668) date almost all the monuments at Mamallapuram. Later the chisel was discarded under Rajasimha (c. 674-800) and masonry reappeared: the temple Jalasayana (p. 19 top) stands so close to the sea's waves that eventually it will

be eaten away, become a mere outline blurred by the lash of spray. Then in the ninth century, the empire of the Pallavas broke up before the invaders.

Like some strange caravan, the five little monolithic temples or *raths* built by Narasimha I stand in line, carved and chiselled out of a rocky layer inclined from south to north; stone turned into temples with figures of gods and princes side by side (p. 19 foot). The men have a connection with the epic *Mahabharata,* India's Iliad. They bear the names of the heroes of that poem, the five Pandava brothers; nor must we forget the lovely Draupadi, the wife they shared. Long and stern was the struggle of the Pandavas against the enemy who had driven them from their kingdom. At last with divine help they reconquered their land. One of them, Arjuna, being still imbued with Buddhist gentleness, was doubtful whether to go into battle, whereupon Krishna, an incarnation of Vishnu, gave him the advice recorded in the Song of the Lord *(Bhagavad Gita) :* "... Thou hast sorrowed, Arjuna, for whom thou shouldst not sorrow ... The wise mourn neither for the dead nor for the living ... Never was there a time when I did not exist, nor thou. Only the unreal does not exist; the changeless one is imperishable, no-one can destroy the essential spirit. The unborn, the permanent, the eternal is not slain when the body is slain. Pleasure and pain, gain and loss, victory and defeat – hold them all equal. So gird thyself and fight, O Arjuna!" These words are illustrated in the rock at Mamalla-puram. In one of the cave-like chambers Vishnu lies on the coils of the serpent "Endless" (p. 22). Two servants and two winged genii symbolise the power of his four hands. Lakshmi, his consort, kneels on the right, honouring him with the gesture of everyday Indian life, hands joined, head bowed. The god's repose is serene. His sleep, between the dissolution and creation of worlds, is conscious. He knows how to rest on essential substance.

Here too is life in busy profusion. There is a boulder, some ninety feet long and twenty-six high, in which the sacred Ganges is depicted descending to earth. A natural crevice in the centre shows a great carving of that river which Bhagiratha, the hermit king, brought down by his holiness from heaven to fertilize and purify the world. *Nagas* and *naginis,* genii of the waters, wimple in the stream in adoration (p. 18). On the rock wall above are *siddhas,* ideal creatures of the air, and below are monks, yogis and holy men in prayer. The joy of Eden reigns; there are lions beside gazelles, a cat engaged upon spiritual exercises among dancing mice, elephants taking their young to the stream where men draw water for their thirst. Perishable creatures rejoicing, in durable rock.

At Mamallapuram life in its simplicity praises our sister water, our brother the sun, and not without Umbrian undertones. We are reminded of them again in the *Krishna Mandapa,* even though divine gallantries are depicted on the walls of this grotto. The blue Krishna is here in his farmstead. With one hand he holds up Mount Govardhana as a shield against the jealous storms of Indra; he is protecting the cowherds who harboured him safely when his uncle was bent on killing him. Krishna's youth is spent among the fragrance of herds. So the day's labour goes on in the peace that he gives (p. 23): a man milks a cow, the cow licks its calf, a cowgirl bustles in, carrying in one hand water-pots for filling, while with the other she steadies a bundle of fodder on her shoulder. But above, the cowgirls (or *gopis*) are dancing to the sound of a flute—very like the flute that Krishna himself played to bewitch them. So India amorously sings, and the mode is pastoral.

Ajanta

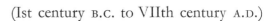

(Ist century B.C. to VIIth century A.D.)

A hill, a seashore, and now the incised rock.

A torrent flows deep in a semi-circular gorge. In the concave face of a cliff polished by rains and waterfalls, galleries open along a walk with steps cut at intervals (upper photograph). For eight long centuries stone-masons burrowed here into the rock, hollowing out chapels and monasteries. Twenty-nine deep caves, many of which are painted and carved: Ajanta, the subterranean city of Perfection.

On the rocky wall, among trailing bushes, effigies of the Buddha go along with the pilgrim, while eagles sail by to the path's farther end. One last image, hand raised in the gesture of teaching. The steps are fairly crumbling in the sun's heat: better move into a cool chapel (*chaitya;* lower photograph). Under ribbed vaulting that copies earlier roofs of wood, a stylised *stupa* is imprinted like a seal with the figure of the Master of Freedom. The frescoes have been talked

of so much that silence would seem best, but there is such pleasure, such a banquet for the eye looming from the darkness of crypts, taking shape among the damp streaks and blemishes on the walls, that they still deserve a few words more. Colours, outlines and shapes challenge the eye not so much to see as to imagine, not so much to imagine as to complete them. One remembers those leprous patterns on walls into which Piero di Cosimo and Leonardo could read faces, landscapes and compositions.

In the niggardly light of a keeper's lamp glimmering arrays of men and animals appear among buildings and flowers. At first the eye wanders confusedly about these faded, damaged frescoes, then scenes stand out, organise and disclose the common hub to it all—the figure of the Prince. Complicated whorls begin to group dimly round this centre—wisdom's light. At last your eyes undertake to read you the legend and story.

A banquet, we said; how else describe this ancient scroll on which parades, scenes of feasting, hunting and dancing cluster round the purified one? Prince Siddhartha had known the pleasures of the court—musicians, concubines, luxury and lechery. These walls allow you to guess what he renounced. While the frescoes picture a conflict between sternness of mind and the sweets of life, between nakedness and riches, truth and appearances, the artists never deny nor condemn the pledges that flesh gives to life.

If a comparison may be made, there is a strange relationship between these frescoes and those which Piero della Francesca painted in the church of St. Francis at Arezzo. The composition of one group definitely recalls the *Visit of the Queen of Sheba to King Solomon*. Here are the same slow movements, the same majesty. The anonymous fresco painters of these caves might well greet Piero as a brother. Notice that long slanting look on the face with heavy turban (p. 25). You will see it again seven centuries later, on faces in the Queen's train. "Great periods meet across time and space," says René Grousset; "an earlier Florence, an earlier Umbria reveal their mysteries here."

Before the Great Departure, Prince Siddhartha had loved the beautiful Yasodhara. "She was like the liana clasping the tree," the poets sang. For her the prince showed his strength of arm and his talents, met the challenge of pretenders. They married, and then he renounced her, together with all his possessions. But Yasodhara is still here, in the rock at Ajanta. Bas-reliefs bring the brief idyll to life again before our eyes. A young man holds a lotus in his hand. A young woman sits at his side. The couch they are sharing is richly draped (p. 26).

The wall paintings in the first grotto show us the Perfect One being assailed by Mara, the spirit of Evil. Mara has launched his forces to lure the prince from the path he has taken towards renunciation. Demons rise, jeering, threatening and howling on all sides. And here are the temptresses, own daughters of the Evil One, wantons that might unsettle any heart, pressing round the chaste youth. Ah, but how lovely their bodies are, how beautiful their gestures! Their hips have the triple sway, and their bellies the triple fold of physical perfection. Such, no doubt, was the way of the courtesans in the palace of Kapilavastu, when the royal youth passed by.

Ajanta is one of the places in India where woman is most charmingly and exquisitely portrayed. The frescoes and bas-reliefs here have been described as "a poem of Hindu women." Strong as the spell may be of the amorous daughters of Mara, there are other figures whose sensual appeal is far more subtle. Entrancing couples are seen in the frames of temple doors (p. 29). These languishing female figures seem to be on the point of giving themselves, but their ardour makes them feel bashful and at the last moment they shrink back. So near and so far, yielding and yet reserved, as much in the flesh and beyond it as Botticelli's nudes. One cannot see them painted or carved on these walls without recalling the words that the poet puts in the mouth of the lovely Sakuntala: "My body hastens forward, but my soul does not agree with it and starts back." A passion too tender, a melancholic desire, soft invitations deferred—such is love's way at Ajanta. And the Emancipated one looks down.

Elura

Elephanta

(VIth to IXth centuries A.D.)
(VIIth to VIIIth centuries A.D.)

Elura seems like a place dedicated to Indian tolerance, a sort of Pantheon where three religions live face to face. Buddhism, Jainism and Brahmanism all give us their stories, symbols and heroes. Twelve of the thirty-four shrines in the rock belong to the first of these, five to the second, and seventeen to the third. There is also a change of attitude, noticeable in the carvings. Though Hindu figures still remind us of Ajanta, still combine human sweetness and intimate grace with provocative charm—Ramesvara's *apsaras* (p. 34, foot) is a sister to Mara's enticing daughters—we are soon confronted with hieratic representations of divine power and energy on the grand scale. Gods tower above the creatures round them; their will to dominate is plain. Siva's drum resounds; he reigns alone in the island of Elephanta. And the pivot of art is the *lingam*. A shrine lies underground inside a temple, and through four doors 'guarded by giant sentinels, the emblem is

revealed—rising, one might think, out of primordial darkness (p. 31). Siva's pre-eminence is expressed in the well-known three-headed statue, sixteen feet in height. His three-fold countenance, seen also in profile on two sides, shows that the earlier Dravidian god has asserted himself and assumed in his being the powers of the other gods: like Brahma, creator; like Vishnu, preserver and protector; and destroyer or rather regenerator through destruction as he is himself. Tremendous as the event seems, it is not the last for Siva. For his *sakti,* his energy, the Great Goddess his Consort, is destined to rise above him, trample him underfoot, and emanate from him in supreme transcendence.

Elura is his throne. Brahmanic cosmology pictures the world as a flat disc with Mount Meru for centre, the peak which is both spiritual—for there dwell the gods—and real: it stands for the Himalayas. Round Meru, "which shines like the morning sun or a smokeless fire," lie in a ring the seven islands and the seven oceans, stretching away to the lofty wall enclosing the world. But Meru is also the cosmic Mount Kailasa and Siva's abode.

33

The great temple at Elura represents it. From a hill nearly a hundred feet high, a gigantic block was hewn and a broad ambulatory cut round it, which freed the mass from the cliff (p. 32). Out of this block men fashioned a temple, tunnelled in to make halls, doorways and corridors, chiselled endless bas-reliefs or worked in the round on the walls; and over the shrine they made the pyramid shape of the roof, stepped up in four receding courses.

The ambulatory is adorned with monoliths—a carved obelisk and elephants. Finally they burrowed into the vertical wall of the cliff and made several superimposed galleries, decorating them too. Thousands must have been engaged on this work in the reign of Krishna I (c. 757-783), a king of the Rashtrakuta Dynasty. Once it was painted, today it is all of blackened stone. The Kailasanatha of Elura is a monument to behold with amazement and awe. Few such works exist in the world. Siva is present everywhere on the temple walls and elsewhere in Elephanta in his complementary aspects. Here he is seen performing the cosmic dance of energy, the dynamic *tandava* (p. 34, above), and wears the terrifying countenance of the *Bhairava*. Elsewhere he appears as the chaste and serious youth, serene and tender, pure lover of a Parvati with downcast eyes, making gift to men of the three sacred rivers—the Ganges, Yamuna and Saravasti—which spring from his tiara (p. 35). His *lingam* is seen being worshipped on the temple walls (p. 13), couples join in *mithuna* (pp. 2, 96) among *apsarases* whose sex sometimes opens like a fig in summer (p. 34).

He even shows himself as symbol of celestial union (p. 33). His right arm rests on Nandi, his vehicle the bull, which also represents his active power. He is Siva—and Parvati too; he is holding the mirror and has the perfect breast of his "spouse."

So on Elura's hill and in the island of Elephanta, the manifold assumes the countenance of the One.

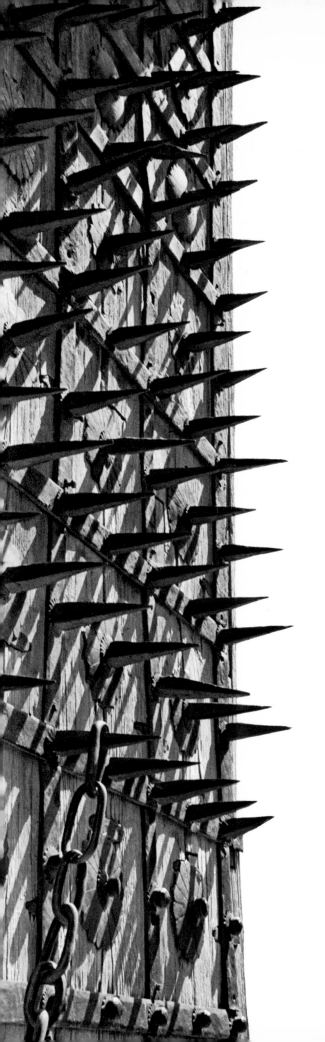

Orchha

(XVIIth Century)

Great is the power of India! It can even be felt and traced in what she is not. Again and again the continent was invaded and suffered at the hands of savage hordes or conquering armies. India absorbed these incoming streams in the silt of her population, and still preserved her soul. Soon or late, she transformed these invaders, or threw them out if they would not yield.

Yet Islam had done its best to break the spirit of India during seven centuries of occupation. The cruel swords of this warrior race were sharpened by fanaticism, by a harsh monotheism. Indians they looked upon as idolaters; they destroyed their images, overthrew their temples, martyred them in numbers or reduced them to slavery. But only the Buddhists suffered severely, because their religious communities were easily hunted down. Brahmanism, being more widely spread in various forms, slipped through the fingers that tried to crush it. It is true that there were Muslims who sought to join the creeds of India to their own. The poet Kabir made an attempt that is not to be ignored, and still more remarkable was that united "house of religion" dreamed of by the Mogul emperor Akbar (1556-1605), to which even Christians were to be invited. The palaces at Orchha, near Jhansi, still stand to record such attempts and give a noble vision of past splendours. Here the domestic Persian style combined with the religious art of the Hindus to create palaces often overlooked by travellers. But only grass wanders over the terraces to-day, and the six-foot lattices on the towers are falling. Sadness broods here, and India draws the moral.

Puri

(XIIth century A.D.)

Once, where Puri now stands, there was only deep forest, but among the trees a statue of Vishnu sparkled. It was carved in sapphire, and its blue made the sea near by look pale. King Indradyumna, who reigned over the land of Malava, heard such praise of this wonderful statue that he decided he must have it. As he did not know where the statue was, he ordered his Brahmans to travel the wide world till it was found.

They searched in vain. But one of their number, Vidyapati, turned east towards a distant land, home of primitive native tribes, the Savaras. There he lodged with a bird-hunter, and soon noticed that this man went secretly into the forest each day to make an offering of fruit and flowers. Vidyapati wanted to go with him, but the hunter refused. Fortunately, however, the hunter's daughter begged and begged, and at last the stranger was led to the place of devotion. The hunter bandaged Vidyapati's eyes to conceal the way from him, then removed the band when they reached the place. And there before the Brahman was the wonderful statue.

Vidyapati had not forgotten to bring mustard-seed, which he dropped behind him unseen by his guide. In this way he was able to find the hidden place himself, and went there alone. While he was admiring the statue, a voice resounded from the sky: "Brahman, take good tidings to thy King! Thou hast found the Lord of the World!"

Soon after the hunter appeared with his offering. The same celestial voice was heard saying: "Oh most pious servant! I am tired of thy flowers and wild fruits! Let me have what I desire: cooked rice and sweet cakes! No longer shalt thou see me in the shape of a blue god. Let me be worshipped henceforth as Jagannath, the Lord of the World!"

Long was Vidyapati kept a prisoner by the hunter, but at last he was free to take tidings to his king. The king ordered his woodsmen to go and bring the statue to his palace. But alas, it had disappeared! Again the voice

was heard, saying: "Oh King, first build me my temple." And it went on: "Thou hast been too proud. Do penance. Then thou shalt be rewarded by Vishnu's image; it will not appear to thee as a blue god, but in the shape of a log of wood, marked with signs by which thou shalt know it."

Soon the waves of the sea brought this log to the shore, and the king commanded that it should be carved into an image of the god Jagannath, who is Vishnu himself. The carvers set about their task, but could make nothing of it. No sooner did chisels touch the wood than they broke.

Then an old carpenter appeared, and he undertook to finish the work in one and twenty days. The king shut him in a cell, and told him that he would not be let out until his work was done. But the king's eagerness was too much for him; he entered the cell before the appointed day. Bolts notwithstanding, the carpenter had vanished, leaving behind him three images which were unfinished; they were roughly shaped and had no hands.

Then the king understood that the carpenter was none other than Vishnu. As for the three images, they represented the god Jagannath and his two brothers Balarama and Subhadra. They were placed in the temple which Brahma himself later came to consecrate.

And that is why pilgrims flock from all parts of India to Puri. Every year in July, the three images are mounted on chariots resembling towers, which are drawn through the streets by thousands of the faithful. The tallest and heaviest of these is Jagannath's chariot. Sixteen wheels carry it, seven feet high. Though there are laws forbidding self-sacrifice, even today men and women are to be seen flinging themselves under the wheels, to be crushed by the god's chariot.

Bhuvanesvar

(VIIIth to XIIth centuries A.D.)

Before leaving Puri for Bhuvanesvar, which is not far away, let us linger a moment to consider a few of the events in Jagannath's legend. These can help us to understand the value given to the image in the Hindu mind. The sapphire statue disappears just as King Indradyumna is about to secure it; the woodcutters come to the forest retreat where it is hidden, and it is gone. Vishnu—delightfully informal! he asks for better fare—replaces it by a shapeless log which will bear three signs to indicate his presence. So the simplest, humblest object has the value of a priceless work of art if it partakes of the divine. Its aesthetic quality is purely relative. Form must combine with manifestation, or it has no meaning for the faithful.

From this point of view artistic standards in the Hindu religion are in no way above those of other religions. A mere stone of phallic shape, a red rag in a crack, can symbolise Siva today just as well as an image devised by rules and norms. All that matters is that it has powers. And to ensure this, believers confer reality upon the image when it leaves the hands of sculptor or painter. A priest "opens the eyes" of a statue and names it during a ceremony, the rite of *prana pratishta*. The faithful gather round closer to pass their own breath into this new, lifeless image. Some perform acts of transference. They make gestures with their hands, as though tearing some substance out of their bodies which they then throw onto the image. Properly speaking this is animation. In India, as elsewhere, beauty hardly counts for the believer where sanctity is concerned. Such was the lesson learned by King Indradyumna. The legend equally reveals the thought that lies deepest in Brahmanism. Remember the vain attempts of the carvers to work on the rough wood. Vishnu alone has the power to express form. In other words, the gods are born from initial matter, the original *prakriti,* existing before their own existence, but it is for them alone to pass from

the uncreated to the created, from that which is not diverse to the diverse, from Being in essence to manifestation. And men must wait for this manifestation. When King Indradyumna goes into the cell before the appointed time, he yields to sinful impatience, as the three effigies show: they have no hands and are roughly shaped.

As with the image, so with the Brahmanic temple which contains it. The temple is not a place *in* which the faithful meet for common prayer, but an image *round* which they gather. This explains the contrast between the wealth of its statuary and the modest scale of the building. It was not till the eleventh century that religious buildings of considerable size were built: the Lingaraja at Bhuvanesvar, for example, or the temple of Jagannath at Puri (p. 38). Here it will be as well to mention the rather simple design and construction of the Brahmanic temple. Lengthwise there is first the porch, which usually stands out and has a few steps in front. Passing through this, one enters a hall—the *mandapa*—which varies in size. At the end of the *mandapa* stands the sanctuary, containing the effigy or symbol of the god, a *lingam* in the case of a Saivite temple. The building may sometimes consist of *mandapa* and sanctuary alone, or even just the sanctuary, with or without porch. For a long period the *mandapa* was covered with a flat roof, made of joined slabs resting on stone beams, supported in turn by stout pillars. Though the walls were thick, solidity always came first. Openings were few and narrow and the lighting was poor.

On the other hand a tower *(sikhara)* was built over the sanctuary. In Orissa, where Puri and Bhuvanesvar lie, this was four-sided and curvilinear. The tower was topped by a rounded disc or torus, boldly fluted. The weight of this superstructure must have troubled the builders, for they made the walls of the sanctuary even thicker and strengthened it with a ceiling.

So the building simply consists of layers of hewn stone superimposed and faced beforehand or in position. No mortar was used. Nor were there any foundations; the temple stands on a base which adds height. This somewhat rudimentary structure was gradually improved rather than altered. The *mandapa* was enlarged, better lit and less cluttered with pillars; these even disappeared altogether. The flat roof was made pyramidal by the use of corbelling, and lesser shrines were built along the side of the temple. And above the sanctuary, also enlarged, the tower grew higher and more imposing.

Bhuvanesvar is virtually a museum illustrating this evolution. The older temples—Parasuramesvara dates from the eighth century—are simplest in design, while those of the tenth and twelfth centuries show improvements. On page 41 it will be seen that the temple of Muktesvara—working round from the left of the forecourt—has a sanctuary and tower above with a heavy torus, then a *mandapa* with a terraced pyramidal roof. In front of the building, which is surrounded by a wall, stands a rounded portico, and behind this can be seen the tower of a sanctuary without a *mandapa*.

But architects were most concerned with increasing the size of the temple. In a hundred years' time proud and imposing structures were to tower above the modest tenth century temples: such are the Lingaraja at Bhuvanesvar or the temple of Jagannath at Puri (p. 38). The original design shows little alteration; in fact Indian architecture may be said to be enlarging on a model. The boldest experiment, also found in Orissa, was to be the temple at Konarak, but here the builders overstepped the mark and the building collapsed; ambition was greater than structural knowledge.

Still, we can scarcely find fault with the modest scale of temples like Parasuramesvara and Muktesvara, for their pleasing proportions are much superior to the grandiose appearance of the giant buildings of the

eleventh century. Their charm, in fact, lies in this modesty. And the quality of their statuary greatly gains because it is used with discretion. It might justly be said that their surfaces are not so much carved as inwrought, in a harmonised and almost continuous design which is admirably conceived for its general decorative and symbolic effect (p. 42). Sometimes it is so rich that one involuntarily thinks of our own Renaissance and Baroque styles. The sculptor's skill—if the point is worth stressing—develops no doubt during the period between the bas-reliefs of Parasuramesvara (pp. 44, 45, 46, 47) and the twelfth century ones of the Rajrani temple (pp. 43, 48). The later work shows a surer, easier hand, and is almost Hellenistic in character (p. 48, right), but it lacks the naive manner-isms and a certain stocky, rustic grace which are found in the earlier figures. Look at the *apsaras* on the Muktesvara temple (p. 49). Her right arm is raised to a branch of *asoka,* a tree which is said to bear fruit only when touched by a girl. Her other hand rests on her belly. She symbolises fertility, as we can scarcely fail to see, and recalls in retrospect the *yakshi* on the gateway at Sanchi.

The Parasuramesvara temple has a delicate and delightful relief showing Siva and Parvati on Mount Kailasa (p. 45). The demon Ravana (time, alas, has almost obliterated him) is underneath them, trying to shake and destroy their

47

divine abode. The goddess seems to be uneasy and on the point of rising. But Siva reassures her. He clasps her to him with his left arm and makes the traditional calming gesture with his other hand. To the right is a figure, half-hidden as if in fear, watching Ravana in his fury, and Durga, a manifestation of Siva's energy, brandishes her sword. This is one of the purest representations in art of loving protection.

In one of the "windows" in the same building are set two friezes in high relief; the upper of the two represents dancing, and the lower one music (pp. 46, 47). May we remind the reader of the significance which music traditionally bears for Hindus? It concerns man in his entirety, and applies to his belly, his thorax and his head. To the belly, regarded as the seat of organic reflexes, it assigns tone, tonal intensity and movements. To the thorax, the conscious centre for pain and pleasure, aversion and desire, it allots melody. For the head, which houses the intelligence, is chosen rhythm, the essence of all.

In the window of the Parasuramesvara temple, bells, flute and drum link music with the three bodily centres of the dancers, but these centres themselves correspond with the three parts composing the cosmos: earth, air and sky. So music and dancing blend with the whole universe and its life.

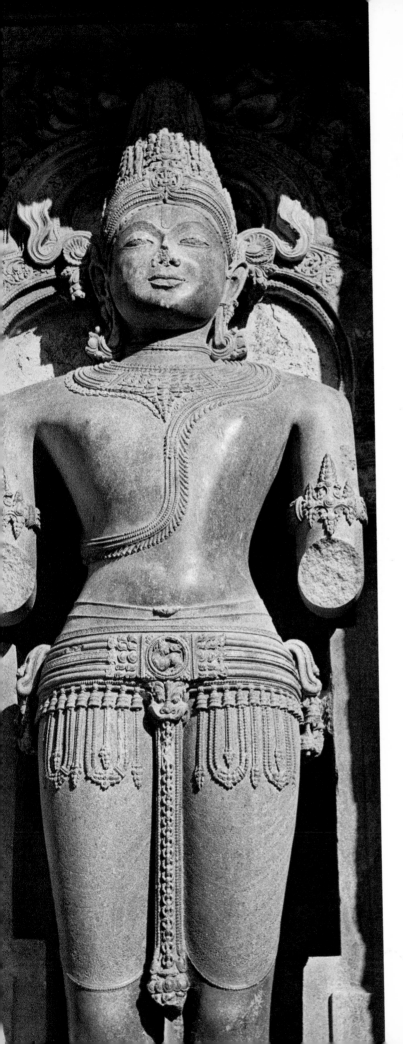

Konarak

(XIIIth century A.D.)

Like a lighthouse echoing to the hammers of the sea, like a dark pyramid on a waste shore, or some caravan forgotten by wandering gods and turned to stone—such is Konarak, temple of the Sun, fallen fragment maybe of that star, with a coating of erotic imagery: caressing, copulation, orgasm and desire.

Twenty-four wheels, carved in stone, twelve on each side and ten feet high, having splayed spokes set with medallions, seem to carry this huge bodywork. Its sides are wrought with figures of gods and men in acts of love, with processions and cavalcades, in a jungle of arabesques and scrolls (pp. 51, 52).

The floor of the vehicle is weighted with massive remains of the first construction. On the left, where only the dark base is seen today, stood the sanctuary. Above it rose a curvilinear tower, like the one on Jagannath's temple at Puri, but more imposing. It was probably 390 feet high (the towers of Notre-Dame-de-Paris reach 225 feet). We can only imagine it rising into the blue sea air. But did the builders build to the top? Was it completed or did it collapse? An earthquake perhaps, or a thunderbolt? Anyhow, cyclopean blocks and great bars of pure iron forty-five feet long lie strewn about, and no-one can say whether ambition failed, whether ruin was sudden or slow.

But the scale we can judge from the almost intact building that stood in front of the tower sanctuary (p. 51, on the right). It is the *mandapa* of the little temples of Bhuvanesvar, now grown into a great assembly hall, the *jagamohan*. The roof rises nearly 230 feet above ground level in three terraced courses; the topmost of these is adorned with guardian lions, and the other two with large statues of the musical hostesses of heaven (p. 53).

The ruins of two lesser buildings lie not many yards away, in line with the central mass: eastwards, a *natamandira* or pavilion designed for enjoyment, as the dancers and musicians on its walls still show (p. 63), and to the west a small

temple. To the south-west stand the pillars of the Ramachandi temple.

A wall enclosed the temple, with four gateways opening at the four cardinal points, decorated with most commanding and expressive statues—horses led by a servant, trampling on an evil genii (p. 54): elephants seizing an enemy with their trunks (p. 55); lions and fantastic monsters (pp. 61, 62).

How did men contrive to build these monuments at Konarak, so far from any quarry, on a sandy shore? What labour, what unimaginable wains conveyed these blocks of stone? How came this remote place to be chosen? For what reasons were walls inscribed in a solitary place with this company of people indulging in pleasures of the flesh?

Let legend first give its answer. Here it is, from the *Samba Purana*.

It was Krishna's desire to be acknowledged as the supreme god, so he devised a plan to make his courage and power known to all: he carried off all the food offered to the other gods. The faithful shuddered at the news. Indra, they said, would not tolerate this daring stroke. But Indra was faint-hearted and said no word. So then all men on earth worshipped the proud Krishna.

The new King decided to change the old order, and all customs, manners and laws. Henceforward one rule alone was to govern men: their desire. They would obey their instincts without remorse. For indeed, said Krishna, delight of the senses destroys time and space. It is ecstasy and bliss. So men were now free from the yoke of faithfulness; like the God they could whisper that the words of a wife are sweet, but not so sweet as a lover's. To please their Master, the priests dressed in saris, painted their faces, and sometimes even simulated

the impurity of each month. There were no desires left ungratified, women proffered themselves to slake the thirst which they contrived to awake. And Krishna himself set the example. In his household there were sixteen thousand one hundred and eight wives or consorts, priestesses of the flesh, and wise withal.

The god had a son, Samba. His beauty, it was said, almost surpassed his father's. But Samba sometimes was in lightsome mood. One day he met Narada the sage, and as Narada was very old, the divine youth could not refrain from chaffing him: "Oh Narada! The laws of Krishna are very sweet, all men in their youth and prime now freely enjoy their pleasure; earth is loud with songs of love-making. What sayest thou, Narada, thou who art too old to do as others do?" And laughing the youth went his way to the bed of his mistresses.

Bitter at heart was Narada. This mockery must be avenged. Next day he offered to take Samba to a secret place where women dwelt, he said, without compare for beauty and passion, who would lie on couches as endlessly as

waves unfurling upon sand. Samba followed the old man. Narada opened a heavy door. And there Samba's eyes beheld such a sight that he thought he was bereft of his senses: women without number were lying naked on carpets of flowers, steeped in their own warmth and fragrance, offering their breasts and bellies and hips to the light. Samba gazed at them. They saw him. They admired his lusty youth. Their desire awoke. They ran towards him. He ran towards them.

But a terrible voice resounded. Suddenly, Krishna was there. And Samba saw the treachery of Narada. The old man had taken him to the inner rooms of the divine palace, and then warned his father. Krishna could not doubt the unworthiness of his son. He thundered. He punished the impious boy: Samba was to be devoured by leprosy, his flesh would rot, his splendid beauty would turn into hideousness, men would flee when he approached.

Samba protested his innocence. He had not betrayed his well-beloved father. Narada alone was guilty. Krishna's

rage abated. His affection for Samba returned. But what avails a god against his own sentences? They must be fulfilled, for he has pronounced them. Samba must be the prey of leprosy. Krishna advised his son to go and live in the solitude of the woods and pray for twelve years to the sun god, Surya.

For twelve years Samba shunned other men, and would not even look into streams to see his disfigured body reflected. He lived in chastity, worshipping Surya from dawn till night and night till dawn. Holier hermit there never was. One day, while he was bathing, Samba saw Surya appear to him. The sun god vanished immediately, but a white lotus grew on the place where he had revealed himself. Samba picked the flower. It shone upon his face when he leaned over the water. And Samba saw that his beauty was restored to him.

He left his retreat, and walked long and far. The flower which he held in his hand guided him. He came to the seashore, climbed a hill, and looking upon the sun without winking, he spoke to the god: "Oh Surya,

who hast saved me and given me back the pride of my youth, here shall I build thy sanctuary. It shall be like the chariot that bears thee across the sky. Twelve white wheels and twelve red wheels shall carry it. I shall harness it with seven horses, all obedient to thy voice. I shall be thy priest. And sculptors shall tell in stone of thy glory, and the life of Krishna and his loves."

What better commentary could there be for the monuments of Konarak than this story of Samba's disgrace and his recovery? For stones here speak with the voice of legend. But history can help to explain certain aspects of an architectural achievement which reflects the political, social and religious life of its day. It appears that the building of this temple can be attributed to King Narasimhadeva I of the Ganga Dynasty (c. 1238–1264). The whole of India was then about to succumb to the Muslim conquerors. They were already masters of the north-west and the north, and most of Bengal. Orissa even was threatened, after lying so long off the invader's path. It was at this moment that Narasimhadeva decided to abandon the defensive. He attacked and was victorious. At once his prestige redoubled.

Konarak testifies to a great reign. A sovereign who has triumphed over formidable enemies requires monuments that will declare his power. So the temple was no longer designed for worship alone. It was a royal palace too, having great assembly halls, pavilions for feasting and dancing. Many of the statues are even warlike in style. Elephants and horses such as these (pp. 54, 55) surely tell of fierce encounters. Konarak, with its gigantic tower soaring above a host of priests and warriors, cooks and dancing girls and slaves, celebrated not one apotheosis but two—the sun god's glory, affirmed in triple majesty (p. 50), and the triumph of his protector, the far-famed King.

Khajuraho

(Xth to XIth centuries A.D.)

Erotic art at Konarak has a rhythmic accompaniment of waves; at Khajuraho, there are the songs of women at their washing and the cowherd's cry.

Temples here rise straight from the fields; primitive ploughs draw lines about them, and the cosmic egg-shapes of their towers stand out against the softer distances of Bundelkhand (p. 4). Looking down from their terraces, one sees the high balance-beams of the wells, and pools where women swathed in violet come to bathe, to wash their children, and fill their copper pots. Quietness is broken only at nightfall. Strange noises then disturb India's darkness—frantic lowings, calls, long bursts of barking. Besides, Khajuraho is only an island won from the surrounding jungle.

A little path leads to the village. It lies away from the modern road and rings to the silver-beaters' hammers, under the watchful eye of a huge red-coloured statue: Hanuman, leader of monkeys, servant of Rama,

protector of peasants. Earth dwellings line a pond which sparkles with pink and white lotuses. A little girl goes by; in her open hand she carries, like a cake, the cow-dung used as fuel. Life was never more traditional, more patient.

On this same spot once stood the capital of the Chandellas, kings of Jijakabhukti. They came from a Rajput tribe and claimed ancestry from the moon. After obscure beginnings, they rose to power in the first half of the tenth century, when Harsha reigned, also Yashovarman his son, who built a shrine for Vishnu—the temple of Lakshmana (p. 82, foot). This, an inscription said, "was rival to the snowy mountains." Dhanga his successor (c. 950–1002) built most of the temples at Khajuraho; his especial pride was the shrine of Visvanatha (p. 74, centre) with a white tower "as lofty as the autumn clouds." Dhanga's grandson Vidyadhara added more great buildings; then the power of the Chandellas declined. They withdrew to their strongholds to try to withstand the Muslim invaders. But Khajuraho flourished for two more centuries; in 1335, Ibn Battuta, the Arabian traveller and geographer, mentions it as a place of devotion where many yogis gathered.

The Chandellas' capital must have contained about eighty-five temples. Twenty are left today, in three groups that lie round the village and extend over a wide area. Sometimes the ruins were used for peasant dwellings. Remarkable fragments are preserved in an open air museum. These and the buildings miraculously left intact help us to assess past splendours at Khajuraho. Architectural originality and a wealth of statuary here undoubtedly provide a magnificent record of Hindu art in the middle ages.

The most typical temples all seek to impress by their height, as inscriptions tell. They are not enclosed, and stand on a high base serving as pedestal, which adds to their elevation. As one moves from porch to shrine, the roofs of successive halls climb higher, suggesting by their contour a mountain chain ascending to its top (p. 82 foot; p. 78). On a front view the temple looks like a peak rising behind its bastions (pp. 64-65; p. 74, right; p. 82, top). The sanctuary tower itself rises out of a cluster of lesser towers reaching upwards. As strict principles govern the architecture, these contours must have symbolic meaning. Though the earlier Chandella kings were Vaishnavites, their successors were fervent Saivites, and their temples may well be intended to suggest Mount Kailasa, proud eminence of Siva's throne.

In its longitudinal axis the temple shows more variety here than in Orissa. The temple of Lakshmana (p. 82 foot, looking from right to left) has a spacious portico with a richly carved ceiling; an assembly hall; a second hall, still larger *(mahamandapa)*; a vestibule leading to the sanctuary, a sanctuary surrounded by an ambulatory. Thus three additions—*mahamandapa,* vestibule and ambulatory—increase the length of the building, orientated from east to west. In design the Lakshmana temple is a cross with four arms forming transepts. The two transepts allow greater width to the *mahamandapa* and the sanctuary, and correspond with four projecting balconies on the sides (p. 75, p. 83). A fifth balcony was built at the chevet. These balconies or loggias admit light into the building and furthermore enhance the decorative effect, for without them the building might appear monotonous and compact, too stiffly held in its mouldings and buttresses, too loaded with its two or three parallel friezes of carvings.

At the four corners of the terrace, the Lakshmana temple has four lesser shrines, small in scale, but this detail does not always recur at Khajuraho. Temples vary according to their size. Some have only one transept (p. 78), others —the Jain temples—have none (p. 71). Some roofs are pyramidal (p. 82, centre). In their general effect the Kandariya and Lakshmana temples combine strength and fine proportions with a rich and skilful use of decoration.

Most of these temples are vibrant with figures in dalliance and possession, but the erotic carvings, like the architecture, show particular refinement. The frank naiveté sometimes seen at Konarak does not appear. The provocative allure of these *apsarases* wears a more studied, precious air which makes them less human and more divine—as indeed they are supposed to be. The *apsaras* statues at Khajuraho are among the most perfect representations of the female form, but in their very perfection they are mannered and affected; some might even be called over-sophisticated. But this does not detract from their charm; the eye never tires of looking at the *apsaras* (p. 70) who is painting her eyelids with *kajal,* the Indian kohl, or the one picking a thorn out of her foot (p. 73, left), and these are only two out of a host that might be mentioned.

The bas-reliefs concerned with physical love are often quite difficult to understand; some compositions come very near to being riddles. Whether this is due to the artists's desire to cover his surface completely or simply to relative modesty we do not know, but the attendant figures helping to support a couple in an awkward posture usually obscure the scene. Take the central group on the lowest frieze of the Kandariya temple (p. 69): two *apsarases,* right and left, are holding up a woman who clings to their shoulders for support. The man below is standing on his head and grips the woman in the crook of his legs; his hands remain free to caress the two *apsarases*. The scene shown on the top frieze is no less complicated, also the one that will be noticed on the lower frieze of the Lakshmana temple (p. 83).

Sometimes style in treatment again becomes naive and earthy. What a difference, for instance, between the reliefs just mentioned and the style of the frieze (pp. 86-87) decorating the terrace of the Lakshmana temple! This band (mutilated, alas, by the hands of time and men) is a film of carnal delights. Though there is zest in the realism, this parade of groups has none of the grace and detachment of *mithuna* on the divine level. Pleasure here is of the earth, earthy; any doubt on this score will soon vanish if the almost frenzied fornication of this frieze is compared with the mystical sensual mood of Vishnu and Lakshmi (p. 67). And the plastic treatment itself has noticeably changed. For the artist followed book and chapter when interpreting divine union, but enjoyed much freedom when depicting mundane pleasures.

Need we repeat that representations of amorous embrace signify the union of separate principles, and are to be regarded as symbolic of oneness with the Divine? None the less, when one looks at this erotic Lakshmana frieze, the mind is teased and baffled. How can such a blunt statement—by no means exceptional, for it can be seen

elsewhere—be reconciled with esoteric meaning? Is there some definite purpose underlying the crude display? One theory (advanced by Mr. Percy Brown) suggests that the figures on the temple at Konarak depict scenes of licence which actually occurred and led to the decadence of the people in that district.

But this is only conjecture which history does not support, and it cannot apply to Khajuraho. Besides, the iconography at Konarak has a special character: it concerns one god alone—Surya, and the sexual act; the scope is limited. At Khajuraho, on the other hand, Siva's pre-eminence did not exclude either Vaishnavism or Jainism, and underlying all three was a Buddhist foundation. So the portrayal of love has a religious background both wide and deep, which is reflected in the variety of the sculpture.

But perhaps we should consider these images—we are still referring, of course, to those which do not rise above crude realism—as provocations for purity? Tibetan Buddhists with a Tantric bias apply certain tests in the course

of initiation to discover whether the novice is virtuous. The lama-to-be is asked to look at paintings of a suggestive nature. If his serenity of mind remains undisturbed, he is entitled to feel that he is on the true path. Sometimes the test is more realistic: the devotee is shut in a room to see women perform lewd dances, or couples miming lechery. Meanwhile a monk observes the patient. If he shows no flutter of desire, he is considered worthy to approach the truth and profess it.

In the same way, perhaps, Hindu erotic images might play the part of tests, and give the believer an opportunity to measure his indifference to carnal indulgence; and they would also show him all the obscenity of perversions, and the great purity of union with the Divine. But surely this explanation is ingenious rather than convincing. What is proper to Buddhism does not agree so well with Brahmanism. In any case, the amorous adornment of temples is never "obscene." Obscenity only comes with ugliness. Now in India, even at the level of sexual realism, erotic art is graced with the utmost plastic beauty (p. 56, *b*). And finally, certain temples—Surya's at Konarak, for example—are too secular in character to allow us to think that the statuary was intended to be purely and simply edifying.

Whether we like it or not, the fact is that Brahmans live in day-to-day familiarity with the sexual act. Among their gods it is commonplace: scurrilous tales abound in the *Puranas*. It represents union between Essence and Substance, *purusa* and *prakriti*. But, as Stella Khamrish says: "This wide and varied range of symbols representing the moment of union forms a complete science and art of love."

The least one can say is that these symbols are curiously ambivalent. Can it be claimed that the *Bhagavata Purana* is just another *Song of Songs*? That the sportings of Krishna and the cowgirls only represent an allegory of the Soul in search of the Bridegroom? This is how Jayadeva, a Bengali poet of the XIIth century, sees them:

. . . With her buxom breasts a full burden, clinging passionately to Krishna, a cowgirl now sings the song of exalted love.
Into the god's face, into those eyes made restless and liquid with love at her caressing touch, another one gazes in fondest, girlish ecstasy.
With eager amorous hand, by the bank of the Jamuna river, in the reed hut where he is gone, another one draws him to her by his tunic.
To another fair one, carried away by delight in the pastoral dance, Krishna now plays on his flute, and the palm of his hand beats time, joins the chinking music of his many bracelets to the pipe's sweet notes.
One he kisses, one he embraces, another fair fondler he strokes, watches a third one's smile, then after a fourth he runs. So he disports himself among this young bevy eager for pleasure.
His alluring spell is on one and all, he wakens to bliss; tender his limbs and dark like a lotus garland, love's joy streams from them. Madly the fair ones kiss him, limb by limb, all all over . . .

We must remember that eroticism ranks as a science in India. Somewhere about the IVth century A.D., Vatsyayana wrote the *Kamasutra*, which gives an exact description of physical love, explains of what acts it consists, and sets

forth its pleasurable varieties. Other works founded on the *Kamasutra* appeared later; in the XIIIth century there was the *Ratirahasya* of Kokkola, and in the XVIth the *Anangaranga* of Kalyanamalla and others besides. All use the method of classification dear to the Indian mind. They are popular compendiums of caresses and postures and give a wealth of advice and information. One learns how a wife may be satisfied and how the prostitute should be treated. They give recipes for magic philtres and aphrodisiacs. Eugenics and the nuptial rites receive attention. They are grammars of sexuality and gallantry, lexicons compiled for every amorous occasion. This is how the *Anangaranga* and the *Ratirahasya* classify women by age and outward appearance:

Until the age of sixteen, woman is spoken of as bala *(child); from then until thirty, as* taruni *(young); from then until*

the years that are counted by the five arrows and the five darts of Love,[1] she is talked of as praudha (ripe). After this time, a woman is accounted to be vridda (old) by the most sage and wise: she is then held to be blameworthy if she enacts all the devices of love, and lovers should always shun her.

The bala *enjoys love's pleasure, which is new to her, in darkness;* the taruni *in the full light;* the praudha *takes her joy equally in light and in darkness, but the* vridda *nowhere: she only robs you of life.* The bala *delights in betel, garlands and so forth;* the taruni *in rich apparel;* the praudha *in a great love, the* vridda *in conversation and marks of respect. Lean of body, too tall for her fat, her bosom low and limbs slack, and very dark—such is the fate of a woman parted too long from her spouse. She that indulges in love continually has a plump body, a clear skin, she is short and firm and her bosom is well developed.*

[1] i.e. 55.

The woman with divine characteristics has a pure, sweet-smelling body, her face is wholly serene, she has abundance of money and men, she is majestic.

She with a man's characteristics is upright in her mind, gifted with cleverness, enjoys being hospitable and does not let fasts exhaust her.

She with the serpent's characteristics often puffs and yawns, has the habit of wandering, sleeps continually, and has an uneasy nature.

She with the Yaksha's[1] characteristics shows no modesty in the presence of respectable people, she delights in gardens, inns and so forth, seeks to satisfy her amorous desires, and is prone to anger.

She with the Gandharva's[2] characteristics is a young woman that knows no anger, wears bright celestial dresses; garlands are her passion, and perfumes, incense and so forth, she is skilled in singing and playing and familiar with the arts.

She with the Pisacha's[3] characteristics is puffed up with pride, eats much, her body visibly burns, she drinks spirituous liquors, eats meat and so forth.

She with the crow's characteristics rolls her eyes continually, makes herself sick with over-eating and falls into vain agitation.

She with the monkey's characteristics has roving eyes, is quick to fight with nails and teeth and her mind is unsteady.

Lastly, she with the donkey's characteristics speaks shameless, displeasing words and is fond of attacking libertines.

Is sexuality a "problem" for the Hindu conscience, as it is for Christians in the West? Here is the answer given by Krishnamurti, who is one of India's present-day thinkers:

[1] Genii, servants of Kubera.   [2] Celestial singers.   [3] Meat-eating demons.

Why is it that whatever we touch we turn into a problem? We have made God a problem, we have made love a problem, we have made relationship, living a problem, and we have made sex a problem. Why? Why is everything we do a problem, a horror? Why are we suffering? Why has sex become a problem? Why do we submit to living with problems, why do we not put an end to them? Why do we not die to our problems instead of carrying them day after day, year after year? Sex is certainly a relevant question, but there is the primary question, why do we make life into a problem? Working, sex, earning money, thinking, feeling, experiencing—you know, the whole business of living—why is it a problem? Is it not essentially because we always think from a particular point of view, from a fixed point of view? We are always thinking from a centre towards the periphery, but the periphery is the centre for most of us and so anything we touch is superficial . . .

What do we mean by the problem of sex? Is it the act, or is it a thought about the act? Surely it is not the act. The sexual act is no problem to you, any more than eating, but if you think about eating or anything else all day long because you have nothing else to think about, it becomes a problem to you. Is the sexual act the problem or is it the thought about the act? Why do you think about it, build it up, which you are obviously doing, with your cinemas, magazines, stories, the way women dress—everything? Why does the mind build it up, why does the mind think about sex at all? Why has it become a central issue in your life? When there are so many things calling, you give complete attention to the thought of sex. And what happens when your minds are so occupied with it? Because that is a way of ultimate escape, is it not? It is a way of complete self-forgetfulness. For the time being, at least for that moment, you can forget yourself—and there is no other way of forgetting yourself. Everything else you do in life gives emphasis to the "me," to the self. Your business, your religion, your gods, your leaders, your political and economic actions, your escapes, your social activities, your choice of a party—all that is emphasizing and giving strength to the "me." And as there is

only one act in which there is no emphasis on the "me," it becomes a problem, does it not? When there is only one thing in your life which is an avenue to ultimate escape, to complete self-forgetfulness, if only for a few seconds, you cling to it because that is the only moment in which you are happy. Every other issue you touch becomes a nightmare, a source of suffering and pain. So you cling to the one thing which gives complete self-forgetfulness, which you call happiness. But when you cling to it, it too becomes a nightmare, because then you want to be free from it, you do not want to be a slave to it. So you invent, again from the mind, the idea of chastity, of celibacy, and you try to be celibate, to be chaste, through suppression, all of which are operations of the mind to cut itself off from the fact. This again gives particular emphasis to the "me" who is trying to become something, so again you are caught in travail, in trouble, in effort, in pain.

Sex becomes an extraordinarily difficult and complex problem so long as you do not understand the mind which thinks about the problem. The act itself can never be a problem but the thought about the act creates the problem. The act you safeguard; you live loosely, or indulge yourself in marriage, thereby making your wife into a prostitute which is all apparently very respectable, and you are satisfied to leave it at that. Surely the problem can be solved only when you understand the whole process and structure of the "me" and "mine": my wife, my child, my property, my car, my achievement, my success; until you understand and resolve all that, sex as a problem will remain. So long as you are ambitious, politically, religiously, or in any way, so long as you are emphasizing the self, the thinker, the experiencer, by feeding him on ambition, whether in the name of yourself as an individual or in the name of the country, of the party or of an idea which you call religion—so long as there is this activity of self-expansion, you will have a sexual problem . . .

The sexual problem is a reaction, and when the mind tries to solve the problem, it only makes the problem more confused, more troublesome, more painful. The act is not the problem but the mind is the problem, the mind which says it must be chaste. Chastity is not of the mind. The mind can only suppress its own activities and suppression is not chastity. Chastity is not a virtue, it cannot be cultivated. The man who is cultivating humility is surely not a humble man; he may call his pride humility, but he is a proud man, and that is why he seeks to become humble. Pride can never become humble and chastity is not a thing of the mind—you cannot become chaste. You will know chastity only when there is love, and love is not of the mind nor a thing of the mind.

The poets of India lift woman to divine heights with their praise. She shines in her full glory in the passionate songs of Chandi Das. He was a Bengali Brahman of the XVth century who renounced his caste for the love of Rumi the washerwoman. His work is infused with the spirit of *sahajya*, a cult in which the youngest and loveliest of their kind were worshipped in rites both spiritual and sensual. Then *sahajya* gave way to *Vaishnavism*, which was more "platonic," and turned to praise of Krishna and Radha his beloved. And when the poet Chandi Das sang the loves of the god and this lovely cowgirl, surely he was voicing his own desire. This is how Krishna pictures Radha for us in the poet's words:

... She wore a sari of blue, and through the front could be guessed her belly's perfection; like lightning her beauty flashed upon me through her veils.
How shall I describe her? Her glances, ever quick in expression, knew no rest. So many and so pretty were the ornaments she wore, that it seemed as if a hundred hundred golden bees had settled upon her.
As she walked I saw that her movements were slow as the gliding of a wild swan.

Never in truth have my eyes beheld lovelier vision; the music of her golden anklets, sounding the fifth note of the scale, was honey-sweet.

In her own thoughts, she passed by, swaying.

Such was the entrancing picture that I beheld.

When she laughed, nectar-drops in hundreds rained down from her eyes.

. . . Her waist was slender as a lioness's, and made me think of the form of the in-tapering dombori *drum.*

Her rump was rounded like a chariot wheel.

On her lotus-like feet danced little bells, circling and sparkling about her.

Her big toes were lacquered and shone far more brightly than the sun.

I could not look upon her body.

. . . .

Oh my friend, tell me, who is this one I know not, with the golden skin?

I saw her bathing at the water's edge.

Listen, oh Subala, my confidant, my tender friend, and hear how she looked, this young creature, as she was bathing. By the bank of the Jamuna river, she was sitting cross-legged in the water, upon the blue sari folded under her.

Her golden necklace was swinging under her naked breasts, that pointed like the tips of the hills of Sumeru.

She loosened her lovely hair, and when she rose after bathing, it rippled all down her back, and darkness, seeing this dusky mass, began weeping and sped away to seek refuge and help behind the moon.

Her bracelets were carved from the sea shell, and shone like the moon's thin crescent rising in a twilight sky.

On the bank of the Jamuna river she walked, wringing my soul with her blue sari, and ever since peace has quite forsaken my fevered heart . . .

Woman's body, the *apsaras's* offering. Face, breasts, belly and rump—all move, with the triple supple
her hips, as the worlds swing in space. She pours out her whole being upon man, weaves about his frame,
irresistible currents round him. (p. 76, pp. 93, 94, right). It is her attraction that draws him towards the
Goddess. And as she heralds the Mother, man yields to her, and so yields to the sovereign Enchantress w
both Beginning and End. What nobler image of woman can be found than this? (pp. 79, 80, 81). She has prostr
herself before the heraldic leogryph; in this manifestation of *Sakti* she acknowledges that energy without which be
would be denied to the very gods.

No couples are seen in the shrines of Christian Occident. They only appear under the baleful signs of maledictio
and exorcism. The first couple are driven out of Eden; they are symbols of banishment and fear, and proclaim the
chastisement of the flesh. But India's civilisation, being both spiritual and sensual, irradiates the union of man and
woman with bliss.

And fleshly love is merged in the rhythm of the monsoons, itself an image of desire and the satisfaction of desire.
Over the land of India spreads the sky, as man over woman.